For Rodin

Best wishes,

Susan

Tao for Now

Susan Corso

DONA NOBIS PACEM PRESS | Earth

Tao for Now is an intuitive translation
of a world-renowned classic.
Any reference to actual persons, living
or dead; events or locales is entirely
coincidental—
if you believe in that sort of thing.
We do not.

© 2012, 2015 by Susan Corso

ISBN: 978-1-937233-25-9

for
Sheriden E. Thomas

Tao

Wisdom is everywhere,
wide awake, on tiptoe.

Josh Billings

Some folks are wise
and some are otherwise.

Tobias Smollett

Teh

How do you get to Carnegie Hall?
Practice!

Anonymous

Table of Contents

Tao

Teh

Coda

Introduction

In ancient Chinese, the character for Tao is a person whose head and body are going in the same direction. I love the idea of a human who is integrated enough to have all of herself going in the same direction.

This is the fourth of four documents in my work on Tao. At first, there were three. The first is twenty-two versions of Lao Tzu's *Tao Te Ching* presented contiguously—this allows immersion in a version; the second is parallel by pseudo-chapter—this allows immersion by chapter; the third is parallel verse comparisons—this allows depth contemplation and the subtlety of word choice to shine. To learn how the fourth came to be, read on, MacDuff.

Process

I did not set out to do a translation of *Tao Te Ching*. Oh, well, perhaps that's not entirely true, but it was definitely in a back-of-the-brain file under the heading Someday. I had just finished proofreading my Parallel Tao Verse Comparisons and decided to re-read it as part of my own spiritual practice. At Pseudo-Chapter 12, I got the inkling of an idea for one phrase in the text. I added my initials at the bottom of the list, typed in and highlighted my version of the phrase, and kept reading.

The next day, an idea for a title for Pseudo-Chapter Thirteen arose in my mind as well as a phrase. I did the same process and before long, in this very chapter, I noticed that an intuitive translation began to arise for every line. I began to type them in, and that, as they say, was *all* she wrote. Or, rather, not all she wrote for I made a file for my own Intuitive *Tao*, figured I'd do two a day till I was caught up and stayed with it. Then, like Alice, I kept going until I came to the end, and then, I stopped. It took two months and fifty-four years.

Realization

At the end of this document, you will find a list of what I call Tao Words. Among them are *Tao* and *Teh*. Translators since James Legge have struggled with English for the untranslatable word Tao. There really isn't an English equivalent that encompasses the entirety of the pictogram.

This time [note those last two words; they are key] I settled on *Wisdom* for *Tao*. As I worked through the rest of the translation, various other words floated through until I realized that any word for *Tao*—as long as the reader holds it in high esteem—will do. The best words are the "intangibles," like Freedom, Truth, Beauty, Justice, Honor, Love, Kindness, Goodness, Wonder, Peace. Try it yourself, and you'll see that I'm right. By extension, then, the Wisest become, the Freest, the Truest, the Most Beautiful, the Fairest, the Honorable, et al.

For me, *Teh* is always and will always be about Practice. The issue isn't: Am I wise? Of course, I am, or, I can be. The issue is: Am I practicing the Wisdom that is mine? If so, excellent; I can expect more Wisdom. If not, why not? The Practice, or Teh, is to get back to inner Wisdom.

Invitation

Welcome to my intuited "translation" of Lao Tzu's *Tao Teh Ching*. I called it *Tao for Now* for a very good reason: this is how I understand Tao at this moment in my life.

Wait, Beloved, it'll change.

Susan Corso, D. D.
Boston, MA
Spring Equinox 2012

Lao Tzu

Tao

Essence Expression

Spoken wisdom is not All Wisdom.
Named wisdom is not All Wisdom.

Celestial, it is Original Wisdom.
Terrestrial, it is Practical Wisdom.

For Celestial Wisdom
—Essence—
     let go.
For Terrestrial Wisdom
—Expression—
     hold tight.

Essence Expression, Expression Essence.
One births another; the other births the One.

All Wisdoms are Wonder.

Relatively Speaking

This planet is grounded in polarity—
no exceptions.

Essence and expression tumble each other.
Ebb and flow tumble each other.
Expansion and contraction
            tumble each other.
Altitude and depth tumble each other.
Sound and silence tumble each other.
Fore and aft, yesterday and tomorrow,
            tumble each other.

Therefore the Wisest live as examples,
taking guided action and
providing heart-felt service
in such equilibrium that words are
superfluous.

Life comes; the Wisest welcome it.
Life goes; the Wisest release it.

The Wisest act for the sake of Wisdom.
Reward is icing on the cake.
The Wisest need no remembrance
and so are never forgotten.

Elegant Simplicity

Choices from within,
not appointments from without,
prevent disappointment.

Misers create thieves.

Deciding we lack nothing,
our hearts remain serene.

The Wisest therefore lead by nourishing ...
       first guts,
       then hearts,
       finally heads,
by calming desires and
strengthening transparency.

The Wisest model elegant simplicity,
living from the inside out.
Contented.

The Wisest live guided action.
They teach it freely
to anyone who asks.

       Practice guided action.
       Contentment reigns supreme.

Full Emptiness

Wisdom sources in full emptiness,
ever-renewing.
Nothing, and in everything.

Sharps are rounded, knots are smoothed.
Glare is prismed. Dust is patty-caked.

The full emptiness of Wisdom empties
fullness over all.

She is the Mother of God.

Impersonal Value

Inner and outer are impersonal;
all creation has intrinsic value.
The Wisest are impersonal, too;
all beings are inherently sacred.

The space between inner and outer
is the pause between breaths.
      Exhale.
Empty, it's powerful.
      Inhale.
Full, it's infinite.

Two ears, one mouth: the ratio matters.
Sound half as much as silence,
      or,
silence double the amount of sound
to stay centered.

Venus on the Half-Shell

Wisdom births
the Divine Feminine.

Access to Wisdom is
the genesis of inner and outer.

Wisdom holds Essence.
Use Her to sustain Her.

Was, Is, Will Be

Birthless? Deathless.
Wisdom
    was,
        is,
            and will be forever.

The Wisest are
subtle and so praise-worthy,
following and so leading,
curious and so witnessing,
detached and so content with what is.

Without agenda, the Wisest fulfill themselves.

Water Works

Energy is naturally fluid.
Energy fuels life.
Life is fluid naturally.

Water works effortlessly.
It falls.
It rises.
It trusts Wisdom without question.

Location, location, location.
Deep, deeper, deepest.
Water has generous gentleness and
     gentle generosity.
Integrity, inspiration. intention.

How do you get to Carnegie Hall?
     Practice.
And what do the Wisest practice?
     Timing.

The Wisest
always fluid,
never stagnant,
content wherever they are.

Danger, Will Robinson

There is always a point of
diminishing return.
Stop.
Don't hold on.
Don't insist.
Don't have a tantrum—or, have one.
No matter.
Things change.

Demanding consistency—the hobgoblin of
little minds[1]—is foolish.
It never works.

Fear for your wealth makes you vulnerable.
Are you strutting, posing, hubristic?
"Danger, Will Robinson."[2]

Instead,
the Wisest do what's needed,
succeed,
smile on the inside.
Move on.

This is Inner Wisdom.

Singularity

Seen properly,
Spirit—
Soul—
Body—
Threefaced Oneness.

Can you let your breath rebirth you with
every exhale?
Can you let your vision clear so that
what-is appears?
Can you love and lead so that you
have no agenda?

When Divinity says *Yes* or *No*,
can you make the choice to yield
every time?
Can you let Wisdom overcome knowledge?

Gestating and delivering,
nourishing and disowning,
achieving without credit,
fructifying without dominating.

This is Wisdom's Essence and Expression
and its Source.

Something from Nothing

Spokes gather into a hub;
the space in the center makes a wheel.

Clay molds into a pot;
the space in the center makes a container.

Doors and windows cut into a room;
the space in the center makes a house.

From Nothing,
      Something derives its worth.

Nonsense

Blinded, deafened, blunted,
eyes, ears, tongues.

Unguided action is a shot in the dark.

The most important things in life aren't
things.

Wisdom ever abides within—
Who would give up Wisdom for whim?

Extremes

Divine detachment resolves extremes.
Why avoid extremes?
It's easier.

Accept what-is.
Relinquish the inner ledger.

All extremes cause fear because
imbalance demands rebalance.

Is incarnation a calamity?
I don't think so.

Wisdom loves bodies.
Therefore,
Wisdom is entrusted
                    to nourish the
                                worlds.

Wisdom Now & Then

Invisible, inaudible, intangible—
Wisdom.

Beyond all polarity,
     Wisdom is the space
          from which Practice
       is birthed.
Wisdom ever returns to Itself.

Wisdom needs no Practice.
Wisdom is beyond front and back,
       coming and going;
          an eternal circle.

What was so of Wisdom
Then
       is so Now
and will be so again
        Then.
This is the Practice of Wisdom.

The Wisest

The Wisest of all times come from stillness.
They are celestial and terrestrial.
They practice what they know.
They practice what they preach.

The appearances of the Wisest are myriad
and do not matter.

The Wisest can be timid and torrential,
cautious and courageous.
The Wisest can be courteous and formal,
crackling and fluid.
The Wisest can be theoretical,
tranquil, and turbulent.
All these at once!

Who can hold stillness till clarity arises?
Who can wait till Practical Wisdom
is the action?
The Wisest.

The Wisest let Wisdom practice itself,
then Practice renews Wisdom
and the Wisest.

Homecoming

Out of Wisdom—Essence.
Out of Essence—Expression.
Out of Expression—Wisdom.
Repeat.

Essence yields to Expression.
Expression yields to Wisdom.
Wisdom yields t...—you know the rest.

The Wisest come home to Wisdom.

Coming home is to follow one's star.
Wandering is to invite disaster.
Homecoming is wiser.
Its fruits are roots and wings

To know Wisdom is to know the Wisest.
The Wisest *yes, and* everything.
To *yes, and* gives one sovereignty.
Sovereignty is regal.
Steadfast sovereignty reveals
        the Divine Glory within.
Divine Glory is where the Wisest abide.
Incarnate or not,
        homecoming is
                an increasing delight.

Sovereign Speech

In the beginning, sovereigns
went about their business and
had no need to draw attention
         to themselves.

Later, there were sovereigns
            who were loved;
still later, those who were feared;
later still, those who were hated.
What changed?

The sovereigns lost trust in the people
hence in themselves.
So, of course, the people
lost trust in the sovereigns.

A great sovereign listens within first.
This sovereignty is awake before speaking.
A quiet word here, a gentle suggestion there,
Voila!
The people say,
"Cool, we did it all by ourselves!"

Losing One's Mind

When Wisdom is abandoned,
rules and shoulds arise.
When intelligence is over-valued,
hypocrisy and manipulation are normal.

When sovereignty of self is ignored,
duty and obedience become the watchword.
When a nation needs to change,
politicians babble.

Simple Elegance

Diminish information, abandon dogma.
Let humanity steep in Wisdom.

Renounce duty, decry righteousness.
Humanity becomes the right stuff,
and does the right thing.

End scheming, abolish greed.
Thieves transform themselves.

These all come from outside inward—
        superficial.
Let Being
        turn into Becoming
                turn into Doing
                        turn into Having.

Simple elegance.

Oooh–Sparkly [3]

Schooling is much ado about nothing.
Overrated.
Does it really matter if it's a jot or a tittle?

Good and evil are labels
        for stories we tell ourselves.
Fearing what others fear
        is just an illusory form of belonging.
        Absurd!

The Wisest choose a different Practice.
        Joy.
        Bounty.
        Grace.
The Wisest are tranquil and unconcerned.
Excess is not on their menus.
The Wisest remain nascent.
They do not forget so they need not
        remember.

Having exactly what they need,
        Being inspires Doing.
    What they have, they use.
    What they do not have,
        they don't miss.

Oooh—sparkly is well and good.
The Wisest also hold *oooh—darkly*.

It is easier to …

                Allow More, Do Less.

Moment-by-moment purpose

                evolves organically from

moment-by-moment attention.

Goals are one thing.

The Wisest prefer Vision.

They may seem inactive,

but *au contraire*.

If I seem different from others,

             it is because I am.

The Divine Mother's breast is my home.

Swirl, Whirl, Twirl

The best Practice is Wisdom,
Wisdom, or Wisdom. You pick.

Wisdom swirls and whirls.
Wisdom twirls till …
Idea makes
        Image makes
                Dimension.
Dimension grows from Wisdom.
Swirling,
      whirling,
            twirling,
Wisdom sources Essence.

Wisdom:
        Life force,
        Our source,
        One course
from
        Above time,
        Below time,
        Past time,
        Future time,
        No time,
        All-time,
        Once Upon A Time,
        Now time
forever and ever.

Amen.

Wisdom:

        then and now,
        now and then.

Before genesis,
after revelation,
EssenceExpressionEssenceExpression
EssenceExpression
        ad infinitum.

How do I know this?
Really? You have to ask?

Wisdom lives in me.

At the Yield Sign

Yield to receive.
  Yield crooked to alignment.
  Yield empty to full.
  Yield rigid to flexible.
  Yield poverty to abundance.
  Yield greed to generosity.
Therefore the Wisest
consciously yield and set an example.

No peacocks they, the Wisest shine forth.
No braggarts they, the Wisest stand out.
The Wisest are recognized
  because they do not glorify themselves.
The Wisest are successful
  because they do not insist on one way.

The Wisest are at peace
  because they do not resist.
Because they do not resist,
  no one resists them.

The ancient adage,
  "Yield to receive,"
is a whole truth.

Yield.
Let Wisdom live you.
You too will become one of the Wisest.

It Came to Pass

Let speech grow from silence.

Gales and floods come to pass.
Got weather? Wait, it'll change.
Nature itself grows passionate, then gentles.
Even more so, humanity.

Therefore:
The Wisest serve Wisdom and are Wisdom.
The Wisest serve Practice and are Practice.
The foolish serve neither and are nothing.

Those who yield to Wisdom become
Wisdom.
Those who yield to Practice become
Practice.
Those who yield to nothing become
nothing.

To serve you must yield.
To yield you will serve.
Trust Wisdom.
Wisdom will trust you.

Showboats

Tiptoeing? Unsteady.
Striding? Tiring.
Showing off? Obnoxious.
Self-aggrandizing? Unbelievable.

Showboats self-promote.
They cannot endure.
Such behaviors are unseemly.
The Wisest eschew them.

Implicate Emptiness

Complete Wisdom breathed æons before
      Polarity.
Omni 4^4, ever-fertile, pregnant with longing,
The Wisest know Our Mother.

I do not know Her proper name
so for ease I call Her Wisdom.
Sometimes, I resort to Pleroma,
Immortal, Invisible, God only Wise.[5]

Since Pleroma means fullness,
implied is emptiness
      and therefore Space.
Emptiness returns to fullness.
      The cycle goes on forever.
Wisdom is full.
      Inner is full.
            Outer is full.
                  The Wisest are full.
In the realm are four fullnesses.
The Wisest are one of the four.

Ideally,
Humankind follows the Outer.
The Outer follows the Inner.
The Inner follows Wisdom.
Wisdom follows Wisdom.

A Matter of Gravity

Gravity polarizes buoyancy.
Stillness polarizes motion.

Therefore, the Wisest keep track
        of their accoutrements.
Arriving even into splendid opulence,
the Wisest are appreciative and unattached.

The Wisest remain centered in Wisdom.
To lose gravity is to lose buoyancy;
To lose stillness is to lose where you are.

The Cost of Giving

No footprint.
No blame.
No bean counters.
No locksmiths.
No binding.

Therefore the Wisest
receive everyone and reject no one.
They receive everything and reject nothing.
This is giving.

So the good person educates the less good,
and the less good is
the good person's example.
Value the educator.
Value the curriculum.
Both teach value.

Don't you see?
The cost of giving is receiving.

Roots & Wings

Dynamism—yang, Magnetism—yin.
Access both to receive anything.
Able to receive anything,
      be the Divine Child.

Knowing yang, keeping yin.
The Wisest become examples for creation.
Living examples
      are grounded and
            wingèd by Wisdom.

Knowing dynamism—wings,
Keeping magnetism—grounds,
Receive everything
      from the Inner.

Eternally supplied by the Inner,
Proportion is the Practice,
The Wisest flourish as simple elegance.

Allowing simplicity, allowing elegance,
all things arise into optimal form.
When the Wisest use
      simplicity and elegance,
            the entire world is at peace.

Wait, Beloved

Action alone is a fruitless path.
The world is ordered,
  not subject solely to action.
Attempting control guarantees loss.

Consider the instinctual:
some lead,
  some follow,
some talk,
  some listen,
some sweat,
  some shiver.
Wait, Beloved. It's changing.
Some grow,
  some shrink,
some birth,
  some die,
some take heart,
  some lose heart.
Wait, Beloved. It's changing.

Therefore the Wisest
are allergic to solo action.
They already know that
  extravagances, extremes, and excesses
foil the holy stillness required
      to maintain order.

Needless Force

When the Wisest work for sovereignty,
there is no need for a
Department of Defense.
Defense, by its very nature,
creates offense,
and we already know what that creates.

War is a waste.

The Wisest begin at the beginning,
go on to the end,
and then stop.[6]

Victory at war is abomination.
There is no need for press coverage.
War begets only war.

The Wisest never use force.
They fulfill their aims peaceably,
Otherwise they change their aims.

Force does not source in Wisdom.
What does not source in Wisdom
sows the seeds of its own destruction.

Warning @ Warring

The Wisest never use weaponry.
Weapons are the tools of violence.
The Wisest prefer the left—yielding.
The warring prefer the right—acting.
Weapons are the choice of last resort.
The Wisest never choose weapons.

Peace is their highest value.
Victory in war is no cause for rejoicing.
It is cause for lamentation.
To rejoice in war is to celebrate murder.
Instead, the Wisest contribute to
        peace in this world.

The Wisest favor the left for
        auspicious tidings.
The right they use for mourning.
The Wisest insist upon the left.
The warring insist upon the right.

Victory in war is a cause for mourning.
Murder, of one, or of a multitude,
causes wailing and gnashing of teeth.
Without heartfelt mourning,
war goes on forever and ever.

Undiluted Potential

Wisdom has no name and
> is always the same.
That sameness is undiluted potential.

When sovereignty follows Wisdom,
everything turns into the best of itself.
Inner and Outer unite to sweet effect.
All shall be well,
> and all shall be well,
>> and all manner of thing shall
>>> be well.[7]

Once Wisdom acts, polarity is.
Polarity insists upon names.
By all means, name what is necessary,
> then cease.
Knowing when to stop prevents entry
> into danger.

Wisdom, rightly practiced,
> is the path of least resistance.

Discernment

Knowing others is smart.
Knowing self is Wisdom.

Mastering others needs doing.
Mastering self needs allowing.

Enough is a decision.
It seeds …
      and breeds …
            Contentment.

Persistence overcomes resistance.
Slow, but steady enhances Free Will.

Those who practice discernment endure,
embodied or not.

The Great No-Agenda

Wisdom permeates everything—
                    everywhere—
                  everywhen.
Wisdom sources everything.
It is eternally unstinting.

Wisdom fulfills its purpose and
instantly
                  lets go.
It gives all things everything,
and does not claim dominion over them,
          or even dominion with them.
Wisdom is so small it has no agenda.

All things return to Wisdom.
Wisdom asks nothing of them.
Wisdom is so great it has no agenda.
Wisdom needs no agenda.
Neither do the Wisest.
Because Wisdom and the Wisest
                  have no agenda,
everything they are, do and have
                  is always great.

Endless Supply

The Wisest follow Wisdom,
and the world beats a path to their doors.
People flock to them
      because of their serenity.

People enjoy savory foods,
             brilliant colors,
                         rousing music.
These are ephemeral.

By contrast,
Wisdom tastes bland,
             appears dull,
                     sounds toneless.
Wisdom is for keeps.

Use it, and its supply never ends.

How Polarity Works

The exhale causes the inhale.

Expansion precedes contraction.
Strength precedes weakness.
Exaltation precedes humility.
Privilege precedes deprivation.

This is called working with polarity.

Gentleness and yielding
          overcome
  force and insistence.

Don't explain what you know.
Just use it, and let it speak for itself.

Governing Peace

Wisdom, never inactive, doesn't act either.
Everything gets done.

If sovereignty would follow Wisdom,
everything would evolve naturally.

Natural evolution will create a desire to act.
Simple Practice will temper desire.

Practice enhances silence.
Silence mitigates desire.
The world governs itself into peace.

Teh

Cling Loosely

Doing requires
      stringent examination of motive.
Being first
      makes doing organic.
Goodness isn't currency.
Practice it, just practice.
The Wisest practice all the livelong day.
This is all that is needful.

Acting as if one were good
      is a step along the path of Practice.
It is not the fullness of Practice.
The Wisest are mannerly
      and need no motive to act
appropriately.

Goodness, rightly practiced,
      propagates Justice.
Those who act as if they are good
      are easily frustrated.
After a time, they are so far from mannerly
      that they punch people in the nose
      even before saying hello!

When the practice of Wisdom disappears,
      goodness appears.
When goodness disappears,
      morality appears.

When morality disappears,
          law appears.
When law disappears,
          ritual appears.
Rite becomes rote
          with the shift of one vowel.
Thus, the seeding of chaos.

Foresight is a minor side effect of Wisdom.
Thus, the seeding of folly.

Therefore the Wisest stay with Practice.
They are not distracted by
          the flower or the fruit.
Their practice is steadfast.
They cling loosely to Wisdom at all times.

Æ Pluribus Unum [8]

From the beginning of time until now,
everything has arisen from
      union with Wisdom.

The Inner, through union, is Essence;
The Outer, through union, is Expression.
The discarnate, in union, are
      holy benevolence.
The incarnate, in union, are
      wholly themselves.
Everything, in union, is alive.
Sovereignty, in union,
      is the flourishing of the realm.

The practice of Wisdom is
      the power of union.

Without Wisdom,
      the Inner loses its diversity.
Without Wisdom,
      the Outer loses its oneness.
Without Wisdom,
      the discarnate float away.
Without Wisdom,
      the incarnate crumble to bits.
Without Wisdom,
      Divine Sparks perish.

Without Wisdom,
      sovereignty stumbles.

Therefore,
      humility seeds nobility;
      lowliness seeds loftiness.

This is why sovereignty does not crow.
It takes lowliness as a platform.
Lowliness refers to roots.
When sovereignty has roots, it has wings.

The parts of anything,
      added together,
            make a whole.
Be content
      to be a part of everything.

Too much success is just as tough
                 as not enough.

How do you know
      that an ordinary stone
         isn't masking
            the glory of a gem?
You don't.

Return Again

Expression returns to Essence.
Quickening returns to quiescence.

Everything arises from Practice.
Practice arises from Wisdom.
Wisdom arises from possibility.

Topsy-Turvy Wisdom

When honor-roll students hear of Wisdom,
    they practice conscientiously.
When average students hear of Wisdom,
    they practice sporadically.
When poor students hear of Wisdom,
    they laugh hysterically.
Wisdom would be suspect
        if they didn't laugh.

So there is an old adage:
Wisdom places light next to dark.
Wisdom places advance next to retreat.
Wisdom places ease next to effort.

The mountaintop seems a valley.
    Purity seems sullied.
Wholeness seems fragmented.
    Surplus seems lacking.
Courage seems daunted.
Abundant Practice seems futile.
Habitual Practice seems useless.
Empowered Practice seems wasteful.
A great space has no borders.
    A great talent matures over time.
A great song comes from silence.
    A great sculpture has no form.
Wisdom seems topsy-turvy.

Every time we seek it,
we think we've found it,
and it disappears.

Yet only Wisdom seeds,
                feeds,
        and breeds everything.

Genesis

Wisdom is Essence hence One.
Wisdom is Expression hence Two.
Wisdom is Everything hence Three.

The polarities of yin and yang
    comprise every manifest thing.
Infinite recipes for yin and yang
    combine to create *chi*.
Harmonious chi—or life force—
    fuels manifestation.

People suffer when orphaned,
                hungry,
                        or poor.
Strangely, sovereignty claims
            these adjectives
            humbly for itself.
Reverse psychology?
Oh, I see.
Gain and loss are not always
what they seem
            at first glance.

The Wisest have long taught this precept:
Do not be fooled by appearances.
            Look deeper!
This is the genesis of my teachings.

Curriculum

Yielding forever overcomes rigidity.
Nonresistance to what-is
  is the best default position.
Guided action is the only wise course.

The Wisest opt to teach in this way:

Silence before speech,
Stillness before motion.

Rich indeed are those who choose this path.

Fountain of Youth

What's your priority?

Fame and money,
  or your well-being?
What do you value most?
   Your stuff, or your soul?
Winning and losing,
  which is your most painful?
Excessive attachment leads to
   exorbitant cost.

The miser is miserable.
The giver is gifted.

Contentment is a grace.

Knowing what is enough in all things,
the Wisest lead long and happy lives.

Empty Fullness

Great accomplishments
      lead to more striving.
Do not forget to appreciate
          what you have already done.
Empty out your fullness
so as always to have more.

The straight twist.
The skilled falter.
The eloquent stutter.

Perpetual motion foils cold.
Serene stillness foils heat.

Embody serenity,
      and you set the tone
          for the entire universe.

Contentment

When Wisdom is in charge of the worlds,
    war horses work for farmers.
When Wisdom is ignored in the worlds,
    war horses work for soldiers.

Discontent is the most painful illusion.
Discontent is the greatest calamity.
The tragedy here is greed.
The core of greed is enoughness.

Contentment arrives to stay
    the moment
    one is,

        does,

            and has
    enough.

Don't Just Do Something, Sit There

The worlds are knowable
    from the inside out.

A window isn't necessary to
    behold the Inner.
The more information,
    the less one knows.

Therefore the Wisest stay within and know.
They need not behold to see.
They do nothing and finish everything.

Attraction

The smartest add something every day.
The Wisest subtract something every day.

Subtract more and more—
arrive at organic action.
Organic action means no striving.
And ta-da!
         Everything is done.

True Wisdom:
         Allow more, do less.

Attraction makes right action.

Reward

The Wisest do not rely on their minds.
They read the people's minds instead.

People are good.
People are bad.
So?
The reward of Practice is goodness for all.

People are trustworthy.
People are untrustworthy.
So?
The reward of Practice is trust for all.

The Wisest live in the world but not of it.[9]
Beloved souls follow them.

Life Cycle

People are born.
People live.
People die.

Three of ten are loyal to birthing.
Three of ten are loyal to living.
Three of ten are loyal to dying.

Why is this so?
Because fear of dying means fear of living.

When fear of dying is the primary lens,
wild animals threaten one on city sidewalks,
and nightmares implode out of nowhere.

When love of living is the primary lens,
rhinoceros horns cannot pierce,
tiger claws cannot scratch,
and lethal weapons do not harm.

Pourquoi?
Death has no entrée there.

Ignition

Wisdom is the Divine Spark of all creation.
Practice ignites the Divine Spark.
Breath exhorts it into Divine Flame.

Nature makes the shapes of creation.
Nurture grows the forms of creation.
Thus all things naturally
honor Wisdom and
value Practice.

Glorifying Wisdom! Treasuring Practice!
These arise from within.
The Wisdom within makes it so.
So Wisdom seeds all things.
Practice sustains all things …
from cradle to grave.

Creating without agenda,
giving without expectation,
guiding without willfulness—
this is
Profound Practice.

Brightening the Dark

Wisdom is the Mother of the World.
When we know the Mother,
we know the children.
Once we know the children,
we return to the Mother.
Knowing Mother Wisdom keeps us safe.

Hush. Be still.
A simple life is carefree.
Gab. Keep busy.
A complex life is careworn.

Attend to detail to be clear.
Surrender to be strong.

Radiance turns and returns
      again and again
          to the Inner Light.

Inner Light brightens darkness.
This is Divine Glory.

If I Ruled the World

If I ruled the world,
there would be only one path.
     Wisdom.
Or, rather, practicing Wisdom.

My only fear? Willfulness.
Wisdom is simple and elegant.
Humanity gets side-tracked easily.

Public buildings are fussy.
Weedy fields are tangled.
Grocery shelves are barren.

The elite wear fancy clothes,
     bear arms, overeat,
     and over-medicate.
They accumulate things and wealth
     and tell themselves
     it is their right in life.
This is inequitable distribution.

Living like this is a crime.
It is not Wisdom.

Wisdom As Itself

The person grounded in Wisdom
    cannot be uprooted.
The person founded in Wisdom
    cannot be lost.
Truly taught, generations honor Wisdom
    into eternity.

Wisdom, in the soul, makes practice bear fruit.
Wisdom, in the family,
    makes wealth bear interest.
Wisdom, in the community,
    makes practice lifelong.
Wisdom, in the country,
    makes peace take root.
Wisdom, in the world,
    makes prosperity common.

Thus Wisdom, rightly held, is
  everywhere and everywhen.
Watch the soul,
  the family,
    the community,
      the country,
        the world.
Each expresses Wisdom as itself.

How do I know this is true?
Because it is so inside me.

Mysterious Practice

The Practice of Wisdom makes
  all things new.
The childlike aren't stung by scorpions,
  attacked by lions,
    or seized by hawks.

Soft bones, supple muscles,
  the innocent grasps and holds on.
Knowing nothing of yin/yang polarity,
  the innocent exudes vitality itself.
Babies are in such perfect harmony
that even an all-day cry
doesn't make a little one hoarse.

Perfect harmony is everlasting.
To know it is always to be clear.
To be clear is enlightenment.
To be enlightened,
  let the breath breathe you.
Just breathe until the breath stops.
  Then let go.

Manipulating Wisdom leads to sorrow.
Don't even think about it.

Finders Keepers

Finders wait to speak.
Seekers speak to find.

Observe silence.
Honor stillness.
Pause before action.
Be fearless of the future.
Modulate your light.
Meet less-light where it is.
This is the Mystic Yes.

The Wisest hold the balance.
    They do not judge.
    They do not label.
    They do not profit.
    They do not lose.
    They do not praise.
    They do not blame.

The Wisest graduate
    from seeking
        to finding
            to keeping.
They are the treasures of the worlds.

Do the Right Thing

To win a realm, use integrity.
To win a war, don't start one.
To win the world, let the world be.

Why? That's easy.
The more restriction, the more inadequacy.
The more inadequacy, the more poverty.
Poverty is never a good long-term strategy.
The more stockpiled weapons,
      the more fear people have.
The more stuff, the more dissatisfaction.
The more rules and regulations,
      the more crime.

Therefore the Wisest say,
"When I do nothing,
      the people reinvent themselves.
I remain at peace,
      and people naturally
           do what is right.
I remain at peace,
      and people naturally
           become wealthy.
I remain at peace,
      and people naturally
           return to simplicity."

Wait, It'll Change

When sovereigns are open-hearted,
                people are fulfilled.
When sovereigns are closed-hearted,
                people are panicked.

Misfortune! Good fortune!
Misery! Joy!
        Appearances.
Wait, it'll change.
You will be tempted to fix it.
        Don't!
If you wait, things really will change.

Thus the Wisest are content to wait.
They are natural change agents.
Their radiance shines from within.

Practical Simplicity

Simplicity is an excellent measure
      for making choices,
         no matter whom you serve.
Already on the path of Wisdom,
the Wisest use simplicity daily.

Simplicity arises from an inner
         accumulation of elegance.

Elegance compounds through Practice.
Practical simplicity overcomes anything.

When you can overcome anything,
         you can lead the realm.
Rooted in the matrix, you will lead for a
         long, long time.

Keep the Mother in your sights.
Serving Wisdom is practical simplicity.

Power With

Ruling a realm is like frying a small fish—
don't poke it!

In a realm centered in Wisdom,
hungry ghosts[10] from the past hold no sway.
Hungry ghosts do not disappear.
They just no longer have power over.

The Wisest do not use power over either.
They use only power with.

When no one uses power over,
Practice returns spontaneously
and frees everyone.

Alliance

A powerful country behaves like water.
By taking the modest position, all things flow to it
      as rivulets to a river,
Converging down to the depths,
      the Feminine Divine.

The feminine overcomes the masculine every time
      by yielding.
Yielding is only possible through stillness.

Whether seeking alliance with a small country
      or a large country,
whether the seeker of the ally
      or the seeker of the alliance,
allies and alliances are only gained
      through yielding.
The Wisest choose to yield without exception.

What a large country wants
      is the same as a small country.
What a small country wants
      is the same as a large country.

Alliance.

For both to ally, both get still and
      receive each other.

Sanctuary

Wisdom is sanctuary,
> the treasure of the good,
> the refuge of the bad.

Just because you have an opinion
  about people, you mustn't reject them.
Opinions are cheap.
Instead, let your beautiful speech and
  kind deeds teach them by example.
You never know. You could be wrong.

So when sovereignty is crowned
  and officials are named,
don't celebrate them
  with tokens of power and wealth.
Instead, show them stillness
  and offer to teach them Wisdom.

Why do the Wisest honor Wisdom
  above all else?
Because through it
> finding is included in seeking, and
> forgiving is included in
> transgressing.

No wonder Wisdom is sanctuary.

An Easy Life

Do what comes naturally.
Act when you're guided.
Work at what you love.
Eat to live. Sleep when you're tired.
If you're cold, wear a sweater.

Attend to detail and hold the big picture.
Respond to whatever comes toward you
        with Practice.

Start the hard things
   whilst they are still easy.
Do the easy things before they become hard.
Simplify what seems complex.

Great accomplishments arise
   from tiny steps.
The Wisest know this.
They never aim for greatness,
therefore they achieve greatness.

The Wisest under-promise and over-deliver.
They know that hard and easy are relative.
As a result, they assume things will be hard
                unless they are easy.
The Wisest are never out of their depth.

God and the Devil are in the Details [11]

What is still can be managed.
What is ahead can be anticipated.
What is brittle can be broken.
What is small can be dispersed.

Deal with issues before they cause trouble.
Order things before they are messy.

A tree that shades a picnic begins
      as a mere sapling.
A skyscraper begins
      as a hole in the ground.
A journey of a thousand miles begins
      with one foot forward.

Those who act to control are disappointed.
Those who grasp to own are empty-handed.
The Wisest act to set things free
      and are delighted.
The Wisest grasp to let things go
      and are made rich.

Trying too hard at the beginning
      means you run out of steam
      on the verge of winning.
Slow but steady wins the race.
Therefore the Wisest do not rush or grasp.

They know that both God and the Devil
        are in the details.

The Wisest pay as much attention to the
details
        in the beginning
        as at the end,
        and so are guaranteed success.

Living Examples

The Wisest of the ancestors who
 stayed true to their Wisdom Practice
 weren't after enlightenment.
They were living examples.

It's hard to rule people
 when they have just a little information.
Lacking the full picture,
 they take misguided action.
Far better to know
 that they do not have the full picture
 and let those who do take guided action.

This sort of action is a blessing.
If ye know these things,
        blessed are ye if ye do them.[12]
Living this is mystic Practice.

Profound Wisdom Practice
        creates living examples.
Living examples pull everyone
        to return to
        the circle of harmony.

To Lead Follow

Water carves a canyon from the inside out.
Thereby fluid conquers what is solid.

When the Wisest rule the people,
  they speak plainly to them.
When they want to lead the people,
  they shepherd them from the back.

In this way, the Wisest
        serve the people they lead,
and they
        lead the people they serve.

Because the Wisest know
        they are servant leaders,
they follow
        the lead of the people to serve them.

Therefore the people
        gladly serve their leaders.
Because the Wisest serve to lead,
        no one objects to their leadership.

Three Pearls of Great Price [13]

The conventional wisdom is:

Wisdom is phenomenal, and,
The Wisest
      (those who Practice Wisdom)
           are phenomenal as well.

Wisdom masquerades as Folly.
Wisdom is too big to contain.
Folly, on the other hand, is easily contained.
That's why Wisdom looks like Folly.
The Wisest play at Foolish Wisdom,
      and Wise Tomfoolery.

They have three pearls of great price:
The first is Gentleness.
The second is Economy.
The third is Reticence.

Gentleness brings the gift of Power.
Economy brings the gift of Abundance.
Reticence brings the gift of Excellence.

Nowadays, humanity tries
      reverse functioning.

They use Power and discard Gentleness.
They use Abundance and ignore Economy.
They use Excellence and eschew Reticence.
This is bass-ackwards!

Gentleness is the action of Wisdom,
Abundance is the core of Wisdom,
Reticence is the worthiness of Wisdom.

The Wisest wear their pearls every day.

This Over That

The Wisest …

>use gentleness over force,
>use quietude over anger,
>use speech over combat.

The Wisest bring up the rear.
They let their people excel.

This is the practice of non-resistance.
Better, this is the practice of acceptance.

The Wisest are aligned.
If you will, Above,
>Within,
>Below.

Or,

>Heaven,
>Humankind,
>Earth.

Befriending Enemies

Skilled strategists say:

It is better to respond than to initiate.
And,
It is better to withdraw than to insist.

This is gathering without dispersing,
   preparing without arming,
   addressing without grappling, and
   befriending alleged enemies.

It is absurd to insist upon having enemies.
Engaging in resistance with enemies
   means I lose what I treasure.
Why would I want to do that?

The Wisest transform their enemies
     into friends.

Words and Deeds

Wisdom words are simple to comprehend,
      and even simpler to practice.
Strangely, comprehension of them
      can seem elusive,
        and practice of them far distant.

These teachings are older than dirt.

Wisdom words carry arcane meaning.
Wisdom practice is a plumb line.
The Wisest are congruent.

The Wisest are seldom truly known.
If you do, you value both
words and deeds.

Thus it is said:

The Wisest may appear modest.
In their cores live untold treasures.

Coda

Well-Being

Knowing that you don't know
is wellness.
Posing as if you know when you don't
is illness.

We must recognize symptoms
before they manifest,
and address them at once.

The Wisest are immune to this illness.
They never pretend to know
when they don't.

It is because they are well that
they radiate
the blessing of well-being.

Facing Fear

What we fear comes right to us.
Fear good? Good gets ya.
Fear bad? Bad gets ya.
Fear is an equal opportunity gotcha.

To deal with fear, there is one option:

Face it.

Facing fear is an individual task.
No one can do it for anyone else.
Where you were born doesn't matter.
When you were born doesn't matter.
Your fear is yours alone.

Because the Wisest know this,
they gladly hold space for each fear.

This is why the Wisest are also sovereign.
Because they have faced fear in themselves,
they can hold space for others to face fear.

Facing fear sets people free.

Catching Mystery

Flaunting is reckless. You can die from it.
Daring is admirable. You can live from it.
Either path, all choices, have consequences.

One lives, another dies.
Why is a mystery.
Even the Wisest say why is a mystery.
Understanding is the booby prize.[14]

The Wisest come to choice from within,
      in silence and stillness.
Silence and stillness overcome all things.
No worry, no hurry. Done and done.

To live from within out is to wield
      Heaven's Net.[15]
What needs catching is caught.
What needs releasing is not.

Rhythm of Life

Death is part of life.
What is there to fear?

Living is the expert on dying.
No one escapes this.

Aspiring to expertise
not your own is
dangerous.

Taxation

High taxes are wasteful.
People go hungry.
Hungry people are angry people.
Short-sighted lawmakers are toxic.

Death is no threat
because
life is the threat.

Hold death lightly,
and
life takes care of
itself.

Utility

In life, suppleness is useful.
Rigidity is not useful.

Living beings are soft and tender.
Dead beings are hard and stiff.
Stiffness companions death.
Flexibility companions life.

Inflexible force loses.
Unyielding trees crack.
The rigid break.

The yielding prevail.

Surplus

Wisdom balances like a good bow.
What is too much is reduced.
What is too little is replenished.
Surplus decreased. Deficiency supplied.

Wisdom's balance is not the same
      as human balance.
Somehow we have got it reversed:
      we supplement
        those who have too much
and
      we deplete
        those who have too little.
Go figure.

Who is able to remedy this
      crazy discrepancy?
Only the Wisest.
They give to the world from surplus.

The Wisest give to others
      for the sake of giving.
They achieve everything
      and need no praise for it.

Winning

Drops of water overcome steel
because they are more yielding.
Submission beats force every time.

Everybody knows this,
but how many practice it?
         Only a few.

Therefore the Wisest
take responsibility
for the infinitesimal to the infinite.
Because they do this,
they are the best sovereigns in the world.

Paradox is to be savored.

Wisdom's Beloved

Even after détente there are
 unresolved issues.
Living well through them is
 the best resolution.

Therefore the Wisest are content to wait
till the divisions live into alignment.
No one wise demands their immediate due.

Those who practice Wisdom
know the Wisdom of this path.

Wisdom doesn't play favorites.
Everyone is Beloved.

Thwarting Desire

Harmonious populations
   are easy to govern.
Even if they have a squillion weapons,
they have no inclination to use them.
Why?
Because they live in surplus.
To live in surplus is to thwart desire.
Having everything they desire,
   they live and die content at home.

Even if world travel is offered to them,
   they stay peacefully at home.
Even if they are prepared for war,
   they stay peacefully at home.

Living simply, they simply enjoy their lives.
What they eat,
   what they wear,
     where they live,
      how they live.

Even if they can hear roosters and dogs
   in the next village,
they stay peacefully at home to live and die.
To live in surplus
   is to be content
     with what is.

Carry On, MacDuff [16]

Elegant speech is simple.
Simple speech is elegant.

The Wisest practice Wisdom.
They are practicers, not perfecters.
They do not claim to be perfect.
They do not aspire to perfection.

The Wisest have no need to accumulate.
They give all that they are to others
      and they receive infinite surplus
      because of it.
Wisdom is accumulated by use.

The Wisest use Wisdom for
      all beings
      and
      all beings
      eventually become the Wisest.
      It's inevitable.
                  Carry on, MacDuff.

Endnotes

1   *Self-Reliance* is an essay written by American Transcendentalist philosopher and essayist, Ralph Waldo Emerson. It is the source of one of Emerson's most famous quotations, "A foolish consistency is the hobgoblin of little minds."

2   "Danger, Will Robinson!" is a catchphrase from the 1960s' American television series *Lost in Space*. In everyday use, the phrase warns someone that they are about to make a mistake or that they are overlooking something.

3   I owe this phrase to Kelly McCormack.

4   -present, -scient, -potent, -available. A seminary professor of mine called God, the "Omni 3." I added omniavailable, hence Omni 4.

5   This is the title of a famous Christian hymn. Words: Walter C. Smith, 1876. Music: St. Denio, Welsh melody, from Canaidau y Cyssegr, by John Roberts, 1839.

6   Slight paraphrase of Lewis Carroll, *Alice's Adventures in Wonderland*, said by the King to the White Rabbit.

7   Christian mystic Julian of Norwich.

8   Latin: "Out of many, one"—a phrase on the Seal of the United States. Never codified by law, E pluribus unum was considered a de facto motto of the United States until 1956 when Congress passed an act adopting "In God We Trust" as the official motto.

9 Christian Scripture, Gospel According to St. John 15:19.

10 Buddhist concept; to wit, unfinished business from the past.

11 God is in the details" has been attributed to a number of different individuals, most notably German-born architect Ludwig Mies van der Rohe (1886-1969). "The Devil is in the details" has been attributed to Ambrose Bierce (1842-1913). Both are, perhaps, true.

12 Christian Scripture, Gospel According to St. John 13:17.

13 "A pearl of great price" is from Christian Scripture; Matthew 13: 45-46.

14 Aphorism of Werner Erhard, founder of EST.

15 Reminiscent of Hinduism's Indra's Net, or Traditional Chinese Medicine: the web that has no weaver.

16 The actual quote is "Lay on, Macduff ...." It's from Shakespeare's *Macbeth* and are the title character's last words. The quote is often mistaken as "Lead" or "Carry."

Tao Words

Nearly every *Tao* translator, either in introductions they write, or introductions written by others, mentions what I have come to call *Tao* Words. Tao Words are words used in most, if not all, of the translations. Among them are: Lao Tzu, Tao, Teh or Te, Ching or King, the Sage. I also include in Tao Words Tao concepts like wu-wei and return.

Lao Tzu

My favorite is **Wise Child** or **Ancient Child**, as I wrote in *The Huffington Post*.

Mythology

Old Long Ear [the literal translation of the entirety of Lao Tzu's given names] speaks to me of the role of a prophet: one who reports what s/he hears. It makes sense to me as I am clairaudient.

Titles

The Classic of Being and Doing was my first stab at translating *Tao Te Ching*. Now, I'd say **The Wisdom Practice Workbook**. Wait, it'll change.

Subtitles

A Manual for Peacemaking & Peacekeeping was my first attempt.

Tao

Being is one option. **Wisdom** is the one I chose this time. (See Introduction.)

Teh or Te

Doing is one option. **Practice** is the one I chose this time. (See Introduction.)

Ching or King

Classic is my first thought.

The Sage

The Regal or **The Royal** or **The Whole Person** were my first thoughts. I decided **The Wisest** suited better for this version. I liked the plural and needing to choose no particular (read: gender-biased) pronoun.

Absolute

Divinity is one choice. I used **Divine Feminine** more this time.

Kingdom

The Realm or **Circle of Influence** were possibilities. I settled on **Realm** this time.

Wu-wei

The Zone worked for me. I settled on **Guided Action**.

Return

Cycles or **Cycling** were options. I used mostly **Return** in this version.

Gratitudes

Sam Adelman, for producing the album
Amy Bowles Bellamy, for the inspired music on the album
Find her work at: www.amybowlesbellamy.com
Antony Corso, for the lovely tree on the book cover
Find his work at: www.acorso.com
Ray Curenton, for design expertise
Tim Dillinger, for exquisite book production
Jean Haner, for enthusiastic encouragement
Anastasia McGhee, for assistance with particularly sticky
word choices
Suzanne Rhodes, for Taoist web wizardry
Sheriden E. Thomas, for using the manuscript with her Tai
Chi students, and being an excellent sounding board
Rona Q. Wilk, for on-demand Virgoan proofreading
And, of course,
Lao Tzu, for the original

The Intuiter

Dr. Susan Corso specializes in well-being. She has had a consulting practice for 35 years. A storyteller since childhood, she is known for focusing her clients on the new stories they want to tell, and how to make the changes needed to get there. Susan also consults as a leadership advisor and Chief Spiritual Officer for entrepreneurs and corporations.

Susan's blogosphere writing may be found at Seeds of Change, Stack Street, and *The Huffington Post*. She is the author of a fiction series, The Mex Books, the first of which is called *Oklahoma! Hex*. Susan publishes a free e-newsletter, *Seeds*. As a professor, she teaches and ordains ministers.

She lives in Northern California with the spirit of her cat, Charles of the Ritz. Her mission in life is inner peace.

Tao for Now is available as a recording.
For more information, please visit
www.susancorso.com

To contact the author
susan@susancorso.com

To receive a signed bookmark, sign up for
the mailing list at www.susancorso.com